631ART.COM PRESENTS:

"THE NUMBERS"

A BOOK ABOUT THE WEALTH INEQUALITY CRISIS

BY EDDIE ALFARO

Fight For $15 Minimum Wage

Fight For $15

McDonald's We're Not Lovin' It

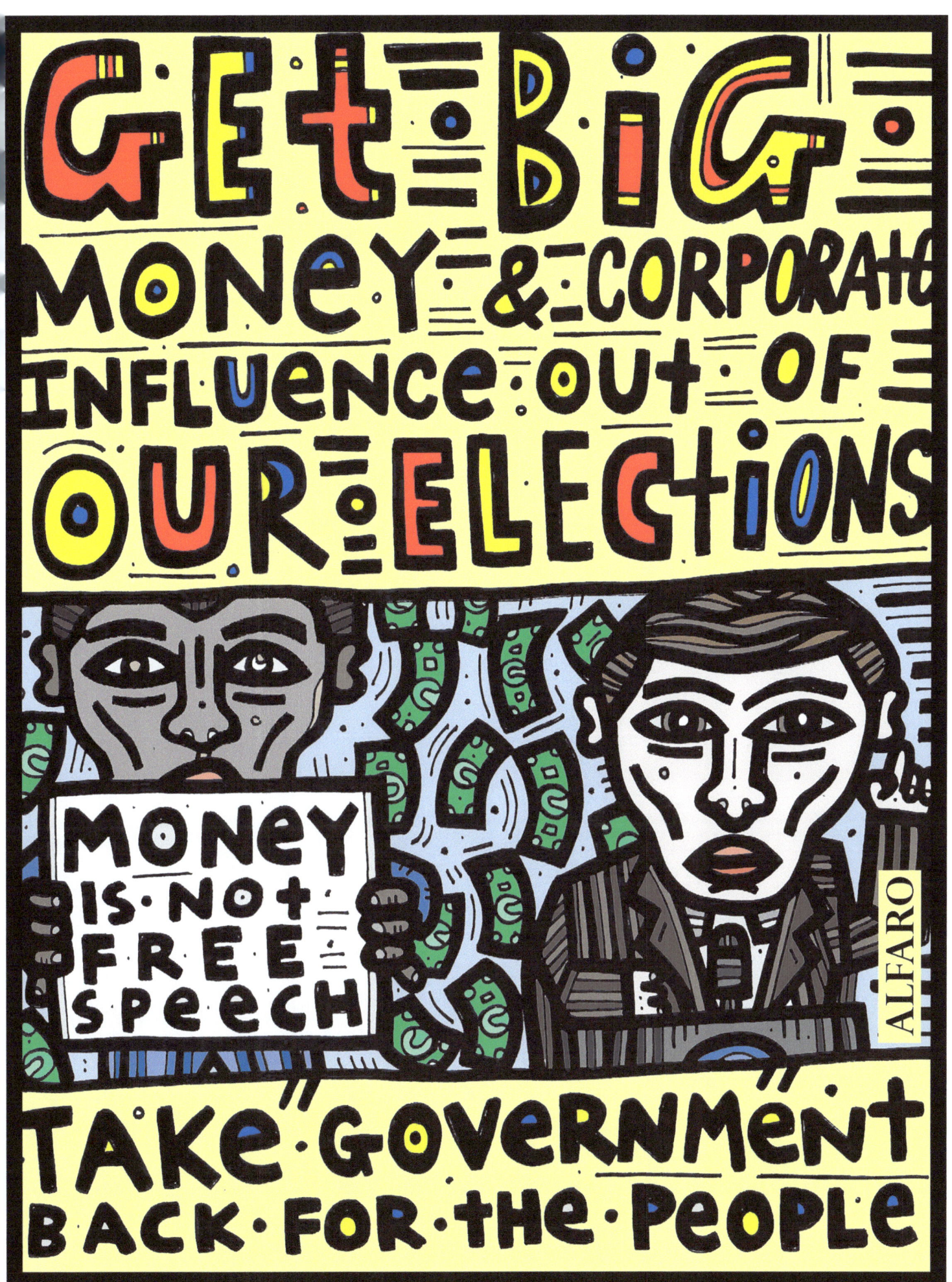

More Money is being spent on US Politics than ever before

Politicians end up reliant on a very tiny group of donors who end up having a lot of power over the political system.

0.26% of the population gives 68% of the money

More than 1 billion people live on less than one dollar a day

780 million people do not have access to clean water

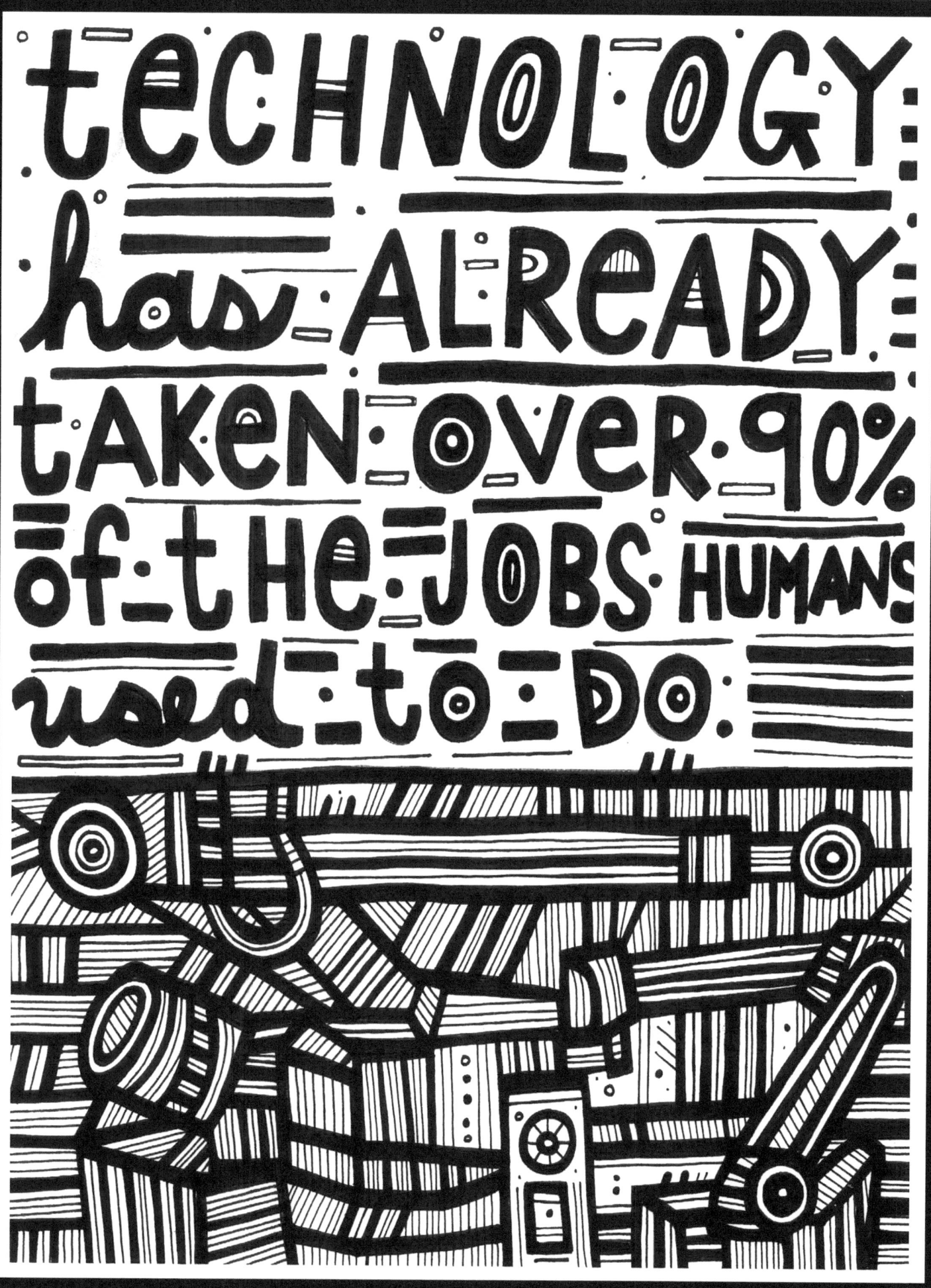

TELL congress to LOWER $ STUDENT LOAN INTEREST RATES

ALFARO

AMERICA'S middle class is SLOWLY BEING 'wiped out'

It's 30% more expensive to be middle class then 20 years ago

All artwork in this book is free for you to use in your non-commercial use. Feel free to share it if you please.

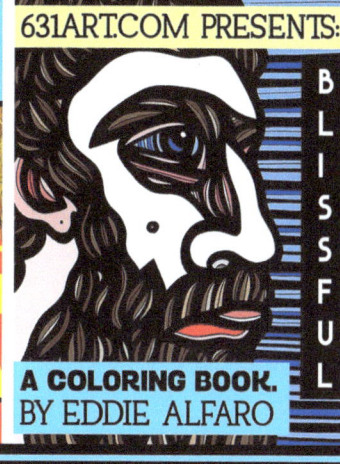
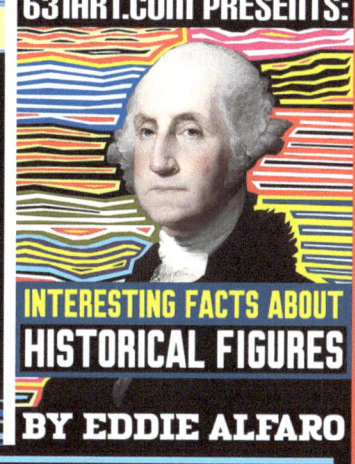

MORE BOOKS AT:

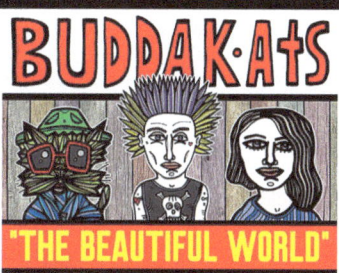

631ART.COM

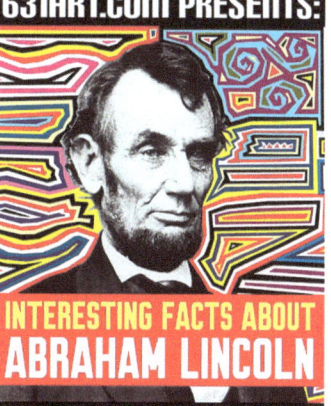
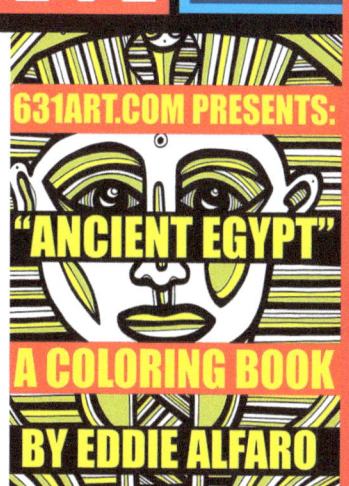

www.ingramcontent.com/pod-product-compliance
Lightning Source LLC
Chambersburg PA
CBHW051201220526
45473CB00003B/855